"Drugs really are great...but God is better."

A Search for Light

Alex Marshall

Preface, Jeff Hood

Preface

I ain't never messed with no drugs. In the moments I might have, I think I lacked the courage. Regardless of my experiences, I can tell you that Alex Marshall had the courage to try any drug that came his way....in fact...this brother daily fucked with some of the hardest stuff out there. While it would be easy to judge him for it...I've decided to take another path. I've decided to listen. So, I guess that's what this book is about...venturing into the unknown...daring to hear complicated truths...choosing to believe that every life is unique. I can assure you that this book is unlike any book on recovery I have ever read. In fact, maybe it isn't about recovery at all. Maybe it is about the divine command to stop and sit with someone who has simply survived. In the midst of all that he has been through...Alex...as imperfect as the journey has been...is a survivor...maybe even an accidental one. It seems that these are the spaces where God finds us the most. Read on!

Rev. Dr. Jeff Hood

Dean, The New Theology School

July 17, 2021

"Drugs really are great...but God is better."

Genesis

Genesis is making me think about how Light is creating the earth as he sees in his image and before Light created earth was there was darkness. It really sets the stage don't it? I fit in the same plan. I used to wander aimlessly wreaking havoc on everything and everyone I encountered. Through the waking the fuck up that took place within me...I've realized that Light is still creating.

Light is the one, the Redeemer. From my personal experience, it reminds me when I chose sobriety that I was reborn. That was my beginning. When Light created me in his image, I believe that was the person I am living as now and not the person I was before. I do however appreciate that Light did all those drugs me...or at least never left me in the process. All the hardships, all the life of crime, and all the struggles led me to my ultimate calling. I have dedicated my life to the Light. Everything that I went through was his plan and I had to persevere for the purpose of me to be able to become this new person with a new beginning. I was formed from darkness just as the Bible describes in the book of Genesis. The earth was void and darkness was over the surface of the deep and the spirit of Light was hovering over the surface of water. I myself was in that darkness, and I was deep in my addiction. Even though it felt good, I was trapped.

It is important as an addict in recovery to learn about the beginning. My story is all about the beginning. It is beginning of this new life of redemption that I am living. I have so many plans that I feel Light created me to see through. I don't feel like that I was created in Light's image to go out and wreak havoc on earth and hurt people. I do feel that the trials and tribulations were necessary because that is what makes my story...mine.

Now I know and better understand in Light's view, in Light's eyes, that's what he wanted me to go through because there are so many people that I can reach on a specific level because of the things that I went through, and I wouldn't be able to reach without the plan that he purposely created for me.

It is incredibly powerful when you think about the nothingness that Light started with. He started creating this earth for us to live on. I think about how before I devoted my life to the light, how I was like that nothingness, there was nothing there. I was essentially an empty body. I had no motivation and nothing to live for besides sticking a needle in my vein to feel good.

I was basically just like a walking zombie. I guess that is the best way to describe it. That there was nothing to me. All I cared about was the heroin or the next hit. It took that to get me to where I am at now. I feel like the beginning of my life sober and free was planned by Light for August 28th, 2019. That is the first time I had ever actually gotten down on my knees and asked Light to come back into my heart and to help me. It brings me back to that day and thinking about just how bad of shape I was in. I was ufuckupsg drugs every day. My wife was about to give birth to our first child. I was trying to get sober. I was trying so hard to get sober up until that day. I just continued to relapse over and over. I was almost to the point where I feel like if there is a Light I need him to help me now. I cannot explain why it was that day or why it took so long. I do not even understand why he made me get to that significant point of desperation. I never wanted things to get so far out of control. That was not my life plan. However, I learned very quickly that Light's plans and our plans do not always match up.

I went through that questioning of faith over and over. I couldn't understand if Light loves me so much, how could he let me suffer for so long? Why could I not possibly love Light and love drugs at the same time? Drugs were my Light. It was the first thing I did and thought of when I awoke every day and the last thing I did and thought of before I went to sleep. I was worshipping dope. I would literally cry myself to sleep at night for all the guilt and shame from what I was doing to support and contribute to my addiction. I was just in survival mode. The physical sickness of not having any dope was so scary that I could not afford to have any emotional attachment to anyone or anything. Drugs made sure it consumed all of me. Yes, I am grateful for the drugs, the trauma, and everything else that came with my addiction. Without it I would not be able to have the faith in him that I have now.

With the faith restored in Light and feeling the Light guiding me I keep hitting barriers. I am not really sure the Light I know and believe in would agree with the constructed religion system that we all see today. I know Light's calling me to lead. Light's calling me to share my glorious victory over the adversary. Due to the path that he chose for me and many others I was not in college or able to gain all the degree's most dominations require you to have to be ordained and lead a church or hold an administrative position. However, the message I have and the knowledge I have is just as important as one someone else taught by professors. Not to take away from these people, but I have a vastly different construct and ability to reach and help people that have had a rough or different lifestyle. I will always claim my calling and my past, it is mine and no one can take that away from me. I just have a hard time with organized religion and the systems put in place within the churches. It really makes it hard for someone like me to climb up and be able to get the same opportunity. Which is strange in the sense that my calling and their calling come from the same Light. I do not believe that Light intended for man to decide who is worthy of discipleship. My reason for explaining my belief is my understanding from Light's teachings. It is his calling, and it shouldn't be restricted by systematic education. Light created us all in his image. If Light is calling someone to do his work, I believe like it is important that you use it. Do not take it lightly if you have that calling and you hear that calling that you take that calling and you run with it, which is what I'm doing. I feel like a new person, everything about me has changed. I feel spiritually whole.

I was glad to get introduced to queer theology because that really opened me up to be able to be accepted. I know Light is in everyone and everything and I know that Light loves me no matter what. From all the things I went through from the stuff I went through as a child and questioning my sexuality for so long. I have family members and close friends that are openly gay, and I kept running into that barrier in religion where they didn't feel welcome at church. That is unacceptable. Light made everyone in his image. It is not mine or the churches or anyone else's place to be judge and jury. We see it too often, churches openly vocalizing anti-LGBTQ theology. We see the same thing with addiction, mental health or homelessness, but it's almost like they want to detach themselves or they do not want to be labeled as being partnered with them. The church as a whole or individuals will "silently" contribute to these causes.

This is my reason for my new beginning. I feel like Light has called on me to be the person that he has created. In order to create a safe place for anyone and everyone to gather and to be able to praise Light in whatever form that they might be or through any labels society has placed on them. Everybody needs a place to feel safe where they can worship. That is important to me. It is unfortunate that these places have not been available and have been the cause of countless division in the churches. When we know Light is love and love is Light. How can we decide who is worthy of his love? Who is worthy to attend our gatherings in Light's name? Sometimes others may not be able to bring themselves to agree with someone else's life choices but to steer someone away from Light is unLightly.

It is okay to let people know that you believe in Light. You do not have to hide. I am happy to scream out my love for Light. Everybody is not going to agree with me or my theology. I am ok with that. There are going to be people who claim to be Lights but will say certain others in society are not worthy of Light's love. My future goal is to create a safe place where anyone can worship, and I am hoping to be able to continue that goal wherever that place is needed. Before I leave this Earth, I pray for everyone to feel safe to worship. To love without limits. It will take some people longer to find that person that Light has created in his image. Some Lights are born and never questioned who Light is. For a lot of us though it's a journey and a continual growth.

"**Drugs really are great...but God is better.**"

Romans

Romans was really intriguing to me. I always felt like committing fuckups was a choice, like perhaps there was something wrong with me not being able to select the correct choice. Knowing now that the laws are spiritual and that I am spiritual and a slave to fuckups is so meaningful for me. In addiction it really applies to me and my experience very well. I have always had the desire to do the good things, but I was unable to do the right thing. I was unable to carry it out. I knew what I wanted to do. However, the fuckupful nature in me as an addict and as a fuckuper would not allow me to do that. I could not get out of the outrageous circle of circumstances. It felt like the same thing over and over. I wanted out of the addiction and way of living so bad. I just was not spiritually sound enough to do it. I think Romans is powerful book of the bible for anyone who is suffering from any type of addiction or mental health illness. You are trying to understand why you are doing the things that you are doing or the things you have done whenever your heart is good. I was just unable to carry out the right purpose or the purpose that Light had put forth for me because I was just living in that fuckupful nature.

In my fuckupful nature, I am also a slave to the law of fuckups. This may be interpreted in many ways, but I interpret this as in my addiction I was a slave to drugs. It was against my basic morality but due to the physical dependency of the drugs I became a slave to them. This is what made me a prisoner and I was held hostage as a prisoner to this fuckups and unable to let these things go. Therefore, the evil in me, the fuckuper in me, is all that anyone could see. There was a war raging inside of me and the addiction was going to win every time. It was the most important thing.

Due to the exhausting nature of this past fuckups and hostage, it has been good for me to be able to work through this book of Romans. I have spent much time making amends with others and more importantly with myself and my Light. The book of Romans really explained to me about my fuckupful nature and how it will always win unless I have a spiritual awakening and am able to fight the fuckups.

I was basically laying down and taking a beating every day because the drugs were more important. It took a combination of things including the gift of desperation of getting in trouble again, the gift of love that I had for my now wife and the gift of the love that I had for my first unborn daughter. There was the combination of all those things and the idea that I was going to lose all those things.

Eventually these things were enough to at least push me over the edge to the point where I was able to allow myself to be open to the aspect of allowing Light as my savior and back into my heart in order to start a new life. I always knew that Light was hanging in the shadows, but I didn't want to accept the Light back into my heart because that would mean having to face my fuckups.

All of this consisted of a lot of change. I knew that if I turned to Light that he was going to change my heart, and he was going to change my ways. I am so glad that with Light's love and guidance I was able to surpass and fight these fuckups and be delivered.

Only then was able to progress and become the Light I am today. That is why I talk a lot about life and just being grateful and thankful for the way that my whole life played out because everything led up to me making this recording today.

All these instances occurred for me to make it to where I am today. Light's plan had to fully play out for me to be ready to take off. There are so many discipleship plans that he had for me.

I knew that only if you had accepted Light as your guide would you walk the path to him. In my mind though I was living in hell. I thought that this is hell on Earth. We do read later though in Revelations that it can get worse.

When you are struggling as an addict you are living in hell every day. Even knowing that you have plenty of drugs to use and you do not have to worry about a physical aspect, the addict is still unhappy. Their heart is empty, and it is just darkness.

And you know that you are not going to have to worry about how you are going to feed that habit. Even when that happens you are still unhappy. Your heart's still empty. It is just blackness. It is just dark. It is just evil and yeah. Having to live like that for years on years on years really changes your perspective on life and on the light.

I still think to this day that I got a glimpse of it. I was in a living hell. I know a lot of people would say to the contrary or that nobody would of course concur with what I am saying but when I was living, I was truly living in hell.

That sickness that I experienced and the hundreds and hundreds of times of sickness that I felt without the drugs in my system is indescribable. I felt that that's hell when you are laying in the bed pouring sweat with every muscle in your body cramping. You cannot eat and you cannot sleep.

You cannot hardly even feel anything it just feels like your head is going to burst. I would have to get out of bed in order to not be sick and go drive around town or the countryside and find boat ramps, parks, cars, anywhere that people would park their cars. People leave their belongings in their cars, and I was good at seeking that out. I cannot explain the feeling. I knew that I was doing wrong and everything I was doing was fuckupful, but I was unable to stop. I am glad that those times are over my life. I lived on the road. I lived for that rush.

That is how sick I was. That is how sick you can get. That is what addiction can do to you. However, you can be delivered from the fuckups. Light can rescue you and Light's always there to rescue.

I cannot tell you when your time can be. I cannot tell you what Light has planned for you. I cannot tell you what path you have to walk before Light opened his arms and says, come home to me. That path is different for everyone. Some people never suffer. Some people from the day they are born everything is right.

Some are brought up in church and do not ever go through those things. I went through addiction and tried to hide the pain of childhood trauma. I tried to block out the memories of being raped in the woods behind my house.

Why me? I can see my mom and dad on the back porch and the boy that was doing it telling me it's okay they can't see us up here. Him saying, if you do this, I'll go play with you. Those are memories that I try to drown out and you know that person ended up dying.

Thanks to Light that I'm at where I'm at today. I pray for forgiveness, and I am in my mind grateful for the path that I went down. Light works in mysterious ways. When he died I did give thanks for letting him and his family suffer the way I did.

I know now that that is not right. I have prayed for forgiveness over, over again. And I've been forgiven because that's what Light does, but those types of memories that you try to hide are what leads you up to addiction and then lead you to the progression from addiction to criminal.

I am just so grateful for all those things that happened because I am like everyone else. I am not scared to share my story. I am not scared to share the truth. A lot of people will tell their stories of recovery, but they do not want to talk about what happened to them when they were a child.

They do not want to talk about the truth or the past. They just want to say oh this glorious Light woke the fuck up me! No. I went through hell. Then Light threw his arms out and said, I will help walk this path with you. Light will not walk it for you but with you. I put in the work, and I am still putting in that work. It is not that black and white.

You do not just pray to Light and say, Light, please deliver me. You can watch videos or listen to other speeches about people saying this is how redemption happened for them. I am telling you though it just does not work like that. Deliver me that from 15 years of heroin addiction, and then you are miraculously woke the fuck up. It just does not work like that. Light is a mighty powerful Light, and he will walk that path with you, but he is not going to walk that path for you.

If you are ready to make a change in your life you will have to be ready to put in the work. You will have to put in the work yourself and open your heart, be honest with yourself and your support network. Be brave to share your story because every time you talk about it a little bit of that power is taken away and given back to you.

Every time I share my story and I give a testimony that power is coming back to me little by little. This is one of the reasons I think it is so important especially with really religious denominations and the way they are constructed that they will find a way to allow people to open up and heal from their past trauma instead of keeping everything unspoken.

We all know that most people suffering from addiction are also suffering from some type of trauma. Nobody wants to share that trauma. A lot of times that trauma is sexual or physical. If we can remove that stigma for people in recovery and say this is a new way and we can all stand up and talk about what happened to us and Light will be here and help us walk through it then we can find hope in recovery. Light is the answer, but we also need a plan and goal to work towards.

I think the more and more I talk about it the closer I am getting to opening people's eyes and opening new avenues for people that are trying to get into recovery. The most important thing you can do is be honest with yourself. Be honest with Light, and if you can start there then you can do it.

Romans tells us that we must overcome that fuckupful nature and continue all the way to overcome that is through the deliverance of the Light. I praise Light that I am at that point and praise Light that I have a powerful support network. I praise Light that I have been in the dumps for the last two weeks.

I had a dear friend pass away on Father's Day from a motorcycle accident. I have a lot of good memories with him. It is hard to continue is times like these. I praise Light that I have the skills now to cope through the trauma. Light walked with me into the doors of the recovery center where I learned these skills.

Light helped me not to die. Light led me to a therapist when I was looking for counsel to help me work through the past. I developed these coping mechanisms to be able to deal with everything. I praise Light that he gave these people minds helping me process through all of this. I could not have done it on my own.

Light is amazing. Light is great. Light will help you. Light designated people to play a specific role in my recovery and to help me grow spiritually and grow a better relationship with him and others.

"**Drugs really are great…but God is better.**"

Corinthians

Corinthians primarily speaks on love. I think the most important aspect is we must love ourselves in order to love Light. We also have to show love and find ways to place that love on other people. Sometimes that is hard to do. The bible talks about loving your enemies, your adversaries, and just trying to love everyone.

I also feel like the first commandment is the greatest commandment.

Everyone knows you should love the Light with all your heart, with all your soul, with all your mind and that is the greatest and the first commandment. I believe Corinthians is definitely addressing our own fuckups and having love in our hearts.

I think that it is talking about how it doesn't matter how much love you have in your heart if you are not doing anything with that and trying to share that Light like love with others then you are not living the way Light would want for us to. If you are not living Lightly at all then you are not representing Light's love to others. If you are a Light and believe in Light, then you are a part of the Light.

We need to show kindness and compassion to everyone so that they may also experience Light's love. We must be kind to one another and love one another.

During addiction I was still a lovable person with a good heart but I was unable to share any love with others. Addiction is selfish and takes away all of the love and goodness in your heart. I let a lot of people down and was very manipulating in active addiction. In that time of my life, others were unable to see the love of Light through me.

I think that it is important for me more now more than ever to show people that are in that type of situation or they're in a similar situation that Light still loves them. It is more important for me now than ever. I feel obligated now to let others know that just because you are struggling, or fuckuping does not take away Light's love from you. He does not love you any less and he is here for you. or been in a similar situation. It is more important for me now than ever.

If we are feeling hatred in our hearts toward someone, we should instead be praying for them. If you have hatred filling your heart than the Light is not filling your heart. I definitely think that love is important especially in today's world because with hate you cannot become the person that Light desires you to be. You cannot love yourself and you cannot love Light.

Being Lightly is showing love and projecting that love on yourself and projecting that love on other people. By projecting love on other people you are projecting Light on them. You don't have to preach at them or talk down on them but it does show a pure gesture of love. This can make them feel the Light in their hearts as well.

Whenever someone feels love in their heart and comes to find Light then they can begin to make changes in their life. It is important to explain to people to love is patient love is kind is does not envy, it does not boast, it is not rude it is not self seeking and it is not easily angered. Love keeps no record of wrongs. Love does not delight in evil but rejoices in truth. I think it is important to show love and it is important do acts of love for people.

Getting on Facebook and announcing that I am a great Light is not a characteristic of pure love. Pure love does not need validation because it is validating in itself. The acts of love are validating within themselves. You do not have to shout the acts of love that you are doing. The anonymous acts of love are more validating.

I like trying to help other people that are in recovery or in difficult situations especially when they feel unworthy of love. I feel like just loving them and not helping them or helping to guide them is not fulfilling your duty as a Light. I feel like I am able to reach them just by praying for them and not seeking validation for or from them. I feel that is the purest of form love. That is Lightly love because it does not need or seek validation.

If you have decided that you want to help someone that is great. If you want to donate money or any other way that you may help to meet another humans needs then you should do that with the purest heart. To keep your heart pure is to keep it anonymous. Light sees your actions and that is what matters. That is not something you should use against a person at a later date. You should not use an act of kindness to hold someone hostage. That is not the purest kind of love that Paul is talking about in Corinthians.

Showing acts of kindness in early recovery are really important for example I was fuckuping being high so much that I began to show signs of having problems with codependency. I was seeking unhealthy validation. It is very important to be able to differentiate healthy and unhealthy validation. It is okay to enjoy the healthy validation but you will not want to get too much validation from the wrong people. You may become a people pleaser in which case it would be very hard to give your attention to your family and Light. I still struggle with that today. It is okay though because I pray to Light every day for forgiveness and for Light to make me a better Light every day.

It is a lifelong journey. It is a continuous work in progress. You will not be miraculously cured. I have been sober for almost two years. It has definitely been a miraculous transformation. With Light in my heart, I was able to get sober. I have to remember to thank Light number one, for everything I went through. I thank Light for prison experience, I thank Light for the drugs, I thank Light for all of the struggles that I went through because it taught me how to be a better person and how to love people, how to not turn my head when I see someone who is suffering, and how to not walk past someone who is in need.

I went from being a person that needed help to being in a place where I can possibly help others at times. As Lights we pretend that we do not see people in our own community that are suffering or within our own church communities that are in need of help. Walking past them is the thing that people tend to do or pretend it is okay because the next person will do something to help them. As a Light community we have to step up and own up. That is what Paul is saying in these letters. That is the Lightly thing to do as a Light and a human, to do these acts of love and to carry out acts of love in Light's name. We should be carrying out these acts of love without any self-seeking desires. We should be carrying out these acts without expecting something in return and loving others for who they are. Light has created these people in his image, and we can love someone that does not love us but who is need without expecting something in return.

I believe it is important that we learn from the readings that everyone is worthy of Light's love. If we consider ourselves Lightly, then we need to look at everyone through the same lens and show them the same kindness and love that Light shows us.

"Drugs really are great...but God is better."

John I

John...Nicodemus is talking to Light and Light is telling him that we must wake the fuck up. When Light says wake the fuck up he is saying you will ask him to come in to your heart and turn your life and will over to him as your guide. In the book of John it really goes in to detail explaining how no one has gone to The light except for those who accept Light. In the book of John it says that everyone who does evil hates the light and will not come in to the light for their deeds will be exposed, but whoever lives in the truth will come in to the light so that it may be plainly lit. Coming from a life of consequences of addiction and battling that evil I did not want to come into the light.

Just because I was not walking the path of Light didn't mean that I did not want to come into the light. I was not equipped to come into the light. I was in fear that my deeds would be exposed. I was not yet equipped with the necessary coping mechanisms. I had not had enough sober time to have a moment of clarity to read the scripture and being able to interpret it for what it says. Light says that everyone is worthy of his love, even me.

Time and time again I asked Light to come into my heart as my Light and savior with the belief that I was going to the light. After having a couple of years sober and living a different lifestyle, not having a needle to use or drugs to use, I was able to come into the light. I was no longer in fear that I would be exposed. Light loves the people that are not coming into the light. Light knows what is in your heart.

After being introduced to queer theology I have begun to understand myself and the person I was becoming. Queer theology is Light is love and love is Light. It has helped me to grow a better experience with Light. I was stuck before. Without embracing queer theology I felt like I did not give others enough grace. I never tried to really understand what others were going through. I believe this can be very specific to the LGBTQ community. I have heard people try to refer this same scripture to them. Regardless of how the church sees fuckups, all fuckups are the same. All fuckupers are the same.

"Light is love and love is Light." We have to love all people and it doesn't matter how someone identifies or what circumstance or situations a person is in. Most of the time those are the people that need our love the most. As disciples for Light these are the people that we need to be reaching out to. We need to engage and love them and show them that we love without limits.

This can also pertain to those who have not been woke the fuck up yet. Whether someone believes in Light or not does not make them any less a child of Light. Light has a purpose and a path for everyone. It is not up to us as Lights to decide when and what that path is or how that path is to be walked. For me it took 33 years before I got to where I am now, trying to walk a better path with Light, walk closer to Light and do as Light did. Light was a healer, Light was a loving Light and he did not seek out the perfect. Light sought out tax collectors, debt collectors, all kinds of groups that were actively fuckuping. We should try harder to connect with the disconnected.

Churches sometimes put more praise on the people that have large donations and not people in need or mental crisis groups that they need to be seeking out. Sometimes we see people with their backpacks and that is all they have. Sometimes those people need Light's love the most. We cannot always provide material things for everyone in need, but we can unpack the negative labels of for example homelessness, addiction and mental illness and show these minority groups that Light loves them just as much. They are as worthy of Light's love as the rest of us.

I decided instead of sitting around talking about what I needed to do I decided to get out there and actually do something that had an impact of the community. I wanted to become part of something bigger than myself. I felt like not only was I accepting Light...Light as my Light and Savior but I was also accepting and believing in the work that Light had called me to do. I began to believe in my calling. I knew that I was doing the right things because I could identify with the people that were sitting on the side of the road, or under a bride or dope sick. I knew that I could identify with these people because I once was an addict too. Light chose me and made me in his image. He made me into an addict in order for me to walk the path that I needed to walk. This is the path that I had to walk in order to have an impact on the people that I am currently trying to help guide toward Light.

I wish that I could reach everyone that is suffering from addiction, mental health or homelessness. I know just from being in recovery when they use the phrase "One day at a time," I say "One person at a time." With Light on my side I am fighting the good fight.

I am able to do these things because I made that genuine change in my life and in my heart. I really embraced my calling. I was able to go from being a criminal to being a contributing helpful member of society, and in particular the community of Blowing Rock, North Carolina. I definitely have flaws, but I know that I am trying and that I am a good person. I can now wake up in the morning and look in the mirror and see a great man, a great father, a great husband and a great Light.

I can still see the person inside of me that was going to my grandparent's house and stealing money out of my grandfather's bible. I know that person will always be there. I know that person will always be a part of me. It reminds me where I came from and where I do not want to go back to.

We should never forget our roots. Light chose me and Light chose my path for a reason. Light knows that I am not going to forget where I came from. Through my heart I will continue to impact the community that I came from. That community is a community of fuckupers and a community of drug users. It is up to me to help connect the disconnected. I have been an addict and I suffer from mental health issues but Light loves me the same. Light lives within me the same way that Light lives within everyone else.

I think it's important to remember that not one of us is better than another in Light's eyes. It is up to you decide if you wish to do the work that Light has called you to do. It is up to you to figure out what your purpose is in life. My purpose is to continue to try to reach as many people by telling my story of Light.

"**Drugs really are great...but God is better.**"

John II

John... I was created in Light's image and that Light created me perfectly. I went out on my own astray from Light and did a lot of imperfect things. Those same imperfect things ended up leading me back to the Light. I have recently been trying to find ways that I can express that. That is when I came to the realization that I needed to be thankful to Light for heroin, cocaine, methamphetamine, and all of the pain and suffering that come along with the drug usage. I am thankful for all of the crimes that I committed and all of the people that I heart. I am thankful for the devastation and chaos that was an affect of my addiction.

I have to be thankful for all of these things. If you take away the drugs, lifestyle and the prison sentence away I do not feel like I would ever be able to have the relationship that I have with Light now. Because of all of those incidences and being able to thank Light for them, it is leading me closer to him and I am able to continue to grow spiritually.

As I grow spiritually, I continue to grow in other ways as well. My love for other people in general grows. I thank Light for mental health problems that I have suffered because I am able to now love those groups of people more. I am thankful for all of the things that have gone on in my life because that had led me back on the path to rededicate my life to my Light and savior. I definitely thank Light for creating these substances and circumstances as many times I found myself silently saying in prayer, "Thank you Light for bringing me closer to you." I was worshipping false idols. Those were my Lights.

For a very long time I worshipped these false idols. This destroyed many years of my life and many relationships and well as destroyed other people's lives. This also affected me emotionally as well as physically. I also want to thank Light for that because it was the means that brought me closer to him.

It is easy for my to be thankful for all of those things now and be able to look at the bigger picture with a mind of clarity and a fresh perspective. No more do I question Light's plan for me because now my plan is Light's plan. I am now able to accept that our plans do not always align. I look at Light as my best friend. I know that he is running the show and I feel like I am his hype man.

I have found ways to be more resourceful to try to connect with Light. For a long time the anger was getting the best of me. I was angry at Light for my situation. The only person though that I should have been mad at was myself. That anger caused me to distance my relationship with Light. A lot of times you read these books that people write, or memoirs, and they talk about how they got sober and their life is so great. You can have this and that and have all of these wonderful things. I don't understand that and do not believe it to be an accurate depiction of recovery.

Recovery is hard. Recovery is work. You do not just get sober and your life magically changes. I do not understand this idea that people get that have not ever been down this road. It is not a cakewalk. Light can give you the tools to help lead you back toward him. I am now trying to walk a closer path to Light and do more of the right things than the wrong things. I know that I have my demons. Those demons will not always be there. I am growing spiritually. I know Light and I know that Light loves me and I am worthy of his love. Sometimes I have to take a step back and think about what Light really is. Light is love and love is Light.

Light was with me when the desperation led me to him. It was a rocky road it was not a paved road, but it goes me there. It is not all fun and games. At the end of the day these are the circumstances that got me to where I am now. I still find myself struggling right now and trying to figure out how to grow. I am trying to grow my recovery ministries. I made a genuine change in my life and dedicated my life to recovery outreach and ministries and to Light . Now that this leadership position at the church in recovery ministries I have a lot of great plans on how to grow this program. I wish it was a faster process and I could reach out to more people. People are dying because of drug use. We can help and we need to help. We need to be out doing what we can.

In order to fully accept and believe John I have to thank Light for everything that led me to him. Not just the good times but the bad times as well.

"**Drugs really are great...but God is better.**"

Matthew

Matthew...I have really been trying to find a way to apply this shit to myself and to my life. I think that by Light asking John to baptize him that it was Light' way of saying that everyone is worthy of his love. From the readings I have learned the Light is trying to teach us that we are all worthy whether we believe in ourselves or not. Light believes in us even when we are at our lowest points. Even if we do not know that we are worthy of his love Light will show us a path. All we have to do is seek that path out.

John at first said to Light "Why are you asking me to baptize you? You should be the one baptizing me." John did not feel like he was worthy to be the one to baptize Light. I feel as though this is Light' way of humbling us. At first John did not feel worthy. Even though John did not feel worthy of this act, he still listened to Light Light and baptized him.

Through queer theology, I am now able to understand that I am worthy of everything in this world and everything that Light is offering to me. I was not previously centering my life around Light. I have done many wrong things and not lived up to my Light given strengths. Through the concept of queer theology I now know that regardless of my previous transgressions and fuckups that Light still loves me. Love is Light and Light is love. It does not matter how much or how little you fuckup because we are all fuckupers. Light was the only perfect being to walk the Earth. Regardless of our fuckups...we are all worthy of the love of the Light.

Lately I have been doing a lot of questioning due to my current life circumstances. I have questioned Light and why I would be on this path I am now. However, I know these questions will not last forever. I believe that it is normal to question the Light.

Light knows everything and he knows that there will be times that we are going to question our faith. I know that he did not write this scripture specifically for me but I do feel like it specifically applies to me and everyone else. Based on life itself we are going to question our worthiness and our worthiness of Light's love. We will also question whether we are worthy of Light's love. Are we worthy of the bad things that happen to us? I have questioned if I am worthy of all the good things that happened in my life and continue to happen due to my sobriety. I was able to come to the realization that it is Light's plan. It took me so long to feel worthy of Light's love. 20 years of that feeling because of my past actions as a child, as a pre-teen and as a young adult.

My family had strong opinions on hanging out with people of other races or dating people of another race. Hanging out or associating with people that were gay was also considered unacceptable. I knew that my Grandfather was the decision maker in the family and we did what he said. He did become more progressive over time. He was learning to love everyone. My grandmother is still alive today and just like him she is now very progressive and accepting in her love of everyone. Sometimes she will ask questions, but ultimately she ends up accepting love.

I have voiced this so many times. I did not feel worthy of love from anyone. So this chapter and these versus definitely impacted me and helped me to feel worthy of Light's love and worthy of everything happening in my life now. All of the things that are happening for me and my family and all of the blessings that Light is giving us I now know that I am worthy of. Of course sometimes I am still bitter towards Light because sometimes our plans do not align. I am fighting this feeling though. This could probably be expected behavior though for anyone faced with similar struggles. I do feel fuckupful for questioning Light and I do feel fuckupful for being mad at Light sometimes. At the same time as being mad or not understanding some of the things he is doing I am also grateful for all of the things he is doing for me and my family. I know that I am really embracing his calling. I am fulfilling his plan for me. I do not know what his full plan looks like yet. It has so far earned me a position in the church and a place in my family.

Light has blessed my family with a home and so I know we will never have to worry about where we will sleep. He has also blessed us with letting my wife be accepted to graduate school to achieve her masters degree to allow her for better future income and allow me to progress in my ministry of reaching the unreachable. We are so blessed to have two beautiful girls and I am blessed to have a wonderful wife. Those are blessings enough. Even though sometimes I do not understand what Light does I am definitely able to look at the blessings that he has given me and feel his love. I know that I am worthy of his forgiveness and I believe that is important when I am questioning him. Now I can pray and repent for his forgiveness. I know that he is going to forgive me for those fuckupss and any other fuckupss I commit. That is very meaningful for me. With a forgiving loving Light everyone is winning because everyone is worthy of Light's love.

"Drugs really are great...but God is better."

Ecclesiastes

Ecclesiastes...I was doing some reflection last night and I started over once again. There is so much power in this story. The scripture really moved me when I read the versus saying for everything there is a season, a time for every activity under the light, a time to be born and a time to die, a time to plant and a time to harvest. I am interpreting that as this is my time. This is my time to live. This is my time to shine. This is my time to give glory to Light. This is my time to step up and answer Light's calling. I am going to make sure that I am aware of what that calling is and that I fulfilling that calling. Light can shout from the rooftops all day about what he wants us to be doing but it is up to us whether we do that or not.

I had a lot of questions when I began my life change. This book answered a lot of those questions for me. I think what really hits home for me is that there is a time for everything. There is a time for me to grieve. There is a time for me to love. There is time for me to hate and there is time for me to ask Light to forgive me for that hatred. I know how important it is to remember that this is Light's plan for me this is not my plan. It is okay for me to get mad at Light and I understand that now. It is okay for me to question my faith even though I am more or less not questioning my faith but asking, "Why Light?"

I wonder if Light loves me why he would put so many struggles on me. I understand that those struggles are part of my story. I try not to think about those things. I just turn them off. I do not want to give the Devil the opportunity to put temptations in my life and the other people's lives that I am influencing. I do not want the Devil to bring me back to the person that I used to be which was a fuckuper, full of anger. I was angry and unhappy with the person that I had become. I was filled with hatred and not filled with love. That is what I am understanding from studying Ecclesiastes. I know now that all of these struggles were timed by Light. Light knew what I was going to go through before I did. It is going to help get me to where he wants me to be as well as being able to come to terms with what he wants me to do. He will enable you to be able to accept Light.

This is what Light wants me to be. I am okay with that. Through life experiences I now have the knowledge to connect with other people. My story is powerful. When I was younger, I prayed to Light several times. Light did not always answer my prayers the way I wanted him to when I was younger. It is only now that I know that Light loved me no matter what I was doing. I know regardless of my past that Light still loves me. I know that all of the things happened for a reason and they just add to my story that led me in to addiction. It also led me into having some serious trauma. I think that is was definitely part of Light's plan to get me to where I am now.

Light has planted the seeds of life and now it is time for me to harvest those seeds and to share my story. It is important to let people know that in Light's eyes your sexuality does not change the way that Light loves you. Your appearance does not change the way that Light loves you. Your thoughts do not change the way Light loves you. Light is love and love is Light. It is important to continue to share this message. I share my testimony all the time about my addiction and how bad I was addicted to drugs. I was breaking in to cars every day to support my drug habit. I think it is important to share the details and an in depth look at the havoc addiction can unleash.

I also think it is important to share in depth details of what led up to my addiction. As a child I was depressed and suffering from other mental health and trauma. It was not dealt with as a child so it only manifested and worsened the older I became. I believe now I can help people that are going through the same thing. Many people in addiction are suffering from childhood trauma and mental health issues stemming from it and my story can resonate with them.

I have been seeing addiction therapists now for over two years and although they cannot formally say it is well known in the addiction community that 3 out of 4 people are also suffering from mental health illness or some type of trauma. I feel like it is probably closer to 4 out of 4. This is another reason I believe sharing my whole story is important and I should not feel bad or ashamed of myself for sharing my whole story. If someone doesn't like my story...that is on them. That's not on me. I feel like it is my time to harvest the seeds that Light has planted in me. It is time to share my story. I am serious about following Light's calling and spreading this love without limits.

People that are in addiction or suffering from mental health issues need to know that someone cares about them. People need to know that there are good Light people that will support them. It is important for them to know that Light is not damning them to hell for their actions, for the sexuality, mental health struggles or even their belief system. Our job as Lights is not to judge. There is nowhere in the bible that Light tells us to go out and judge others. Light tells us to love people. Light tells us to shower these people with love and embrace these people with Light's love. There is nowhere in the bible that it tells us that we should love Tom, Jimmy, and Harry, but Louis over there suffering from mental health and addiction should be damned to hell. Light tells us to love everyone, even Louis. I feel like we should be teaching everyone Light's love and teaching everyone that his love is pure.

After going through the things that I have been through I am actually happy because it has made me be able to have a closer connection with people of various backgrounds. I no longer have to be shy or shame myself for the things that I have been through. I feel these things have only brought me closer to Light. I need to help others to get to where they can have this same connection with Light so that they may prosper. If you are still battling with past trauma you cannot prosper in life because you are stuck just as I was stuck. You feel unworthy. You do not feel worthy of Light's love. You do not feel worthy of loving yourself. Because of this you definitely do not feel worthy of someone else's love. All you feel worthy of is sticking a needle in your arm or whatever you are doing to numb your pain. Addicts in the throws of addiction will do anything to continue this cycle to numb their pain and not have to think about the trauma that they endured. However Light's love offers another way out.

Light has everything planned out, but it is up to us to come to the realization and understanding that Light has everything under control. Pray to him. We do have our choices and Light knows where our heart is. We just have to be sure that we are embracing and answering his calling and that we do it with love and for all the right intentions. Not only do we answer his calling but we share it. It is about getting out there and telling the people that are suffering and getting on their level and making them feel equal. It is about taking action instead of talking and sharing Light's love with all.

"**Drugs really are great...but God is better.**"

Esther

Esther...I was not familiar at all with the story of Esther. I am working on trying to be familiar with all of the books of the bible but I was not familiar with this story at all. Esther and Mordecai knew that in order to save the people that she had to marry the King and be able to persuade the King to save the Jewish race. It is amazing how all of this was planned out. Esther was patient and vigilant. Esther was diligent and resilient. Esther was an amazing person with all of these unique gifts that Light placed upon her. She was especially patient and knew how to present things in a way to be able to persuade people to follow her. She knew how to make things appealing. Esther knew how to get things to go in to her favor. From summarizing the book of Esther and what the verses are really about and relating it to myself I go back to verse 14. This verse says "Perhaps you are born for such a time as this."

This verse has been extremely meaningful for me because it means that Light has put me on the Earth at this very time with these very people and this has been his plan for me. It is so above and beyond any type of understand that I can possibly have. I tried to wrap my mind around how Light has planned all of these things out. However, that is just impossible. What I have been able to do is come to the realization that I was put on Earth at this specific time with these specific people to deal with these specific roadblocks to deal with this specific journey. All of these things are specific to me and had to be done to get to where I am at today, a place where I can save my people.

When I talk about my people I talk about people who are suffering from addiction, mental health, homelessness, with their sexual identities, or anyone that feels unworthy of Light's love. I feel like I need to connect to the disconnected and close the gap for these people that feel like no one cares about them or loves them. My goal is to help them find a place that they can come together to worship and feel accepted and worthy of Light's love. My goal is to make this happen. I do not know if it will be next week, next month or next year. I do know that this is Light's plan for me though. I have prayed and prayed about it and I know this is his plan. I am now trying to bring this plan in to fruition.

From the book of Esther I have really learned what my purpose on this Earth is. I feel like my purpose is to love without limits and I am going to do that every second of every day. I am going to try to share that love that has been shared with me. I am going to try to get more people on board to loving everyone and loving without limits.

"Drugs really are great...but God is better."

Exodus

Exodus... Light is talking about Aaron and Moses going to the Pharaoh and asking him to release the Israelites in the name of Light and allow them to come to the desert to worship him. Of course the Pharaoh initially declines and instead actually increases their bondage and treats them more harshly. He makes their lives worse. This inflamed Moses and he went back to Light and asked Light Why didn't the Pharaoh release the

Israelites? Why is this happening? You sent me there in your name.

Upon reflection of my life I can remember being so heavily addicted to drugs that I could not stop. I can remember being awake for days and asking Light please Light I do not want to use anymore. I would cry myself to sleep at night and tell Light to just give me a chance. I can remember asking Light to not wake me up the next day. I can also remember getting up and saying to myself that I will not use today. Today is going to be the day. Of course by evening time I would be high. I would repeat this cycle and as my addiction progressed into various drugs it was the same thing. I would be asking Light in the same way that Aaron and Moses asked the Pharoah to remove his Israelites from bondage to remove the shackles of addiction from me and allow me to be sober. I was asking for this more and more. I did not want to be using drugs, but I could not stop because I couldn't handle the physical sickness. Any time I would remain sober for a period of time I would begin to go through the physical and mental sickness and eventually it would take over and I would use again. In the end that sickness would win every time.

During addiction I broke in to several cars. I did not even know where I was. I was driving around high on drugs and looking for cars to break in to. People will park at trails and parks. I would find a park and if it was to crowded I would move on to the next one. When I would find some place secluded I would get out and pretend to stretch or get ready to walk, but really I was looking in to cars to see if there were any valuables out in the open.

I ended up moving to Watauga County and breaking in to several cars here. I stole many wallets, purses, and credit cards. I would trade all of these things and money for drugs. I broke into an undercover FBI officer's car, and I was so high that I did not realize it was a police car. I stole a gun, a vest, and all kinds of things. The police ended up finding me which led to a high speed car chase and then foot chase then swimming chase in the river. I was eventually caught and taken to jail.

I was sitting in jail and thinking wow there is no way out of this. My wife was about to get birth. We had just moved here. My wife believed I was sober because I had been going through longer periods of sobriety. There were longer periods between relapses this time. I knew how upset she would be. I was about to lose my wife and our unborn daughter. I was about to lose my freedom. I was about to lose everything.

I did not know that I was going to be able to get out of jail. After about a week of the police taking me back and forth to the magistrate's office and adding new charges daily I finally ended up with a $180,000 bond. Only because my wife was about to give birth that my Grandmother and parents drove from Tennessee to come to get me out of jail.

It was at that time that out of total and complete desperation I made the decision to get help. I told my lawyer that I wanted to get my life together and get sober. When I was released from jail I went to an appointment with the local recovery center here. We had been passing this church daily on our drive home from town. I kept saying I don't want to go this Sunday I will go next Sunday. Finally we went. I prayed to Light so hard in that church that day to remove me from these restraints and let me go from this bondage of addiction.

This time my prayer was answered because I feel like that was when it was my time. I had suffered enough. This was my time. I felt like it was my turn because my story was ready to be told. When I prayed to Light that day I felt an overwhelming sensation throughout my body. This is why whenever I go to church now I drop to my knees and pray because that is what I did that day and it worked.

I felt like that was the beginning. It was my turn. Light answered that prayer. He said okay Alex I am going to release you from this.

So essentially I believe that Light also gave me a gift that day. A gift of being able to effectively reach out to others with my words, my experience, my realness, my honesty, and sharing my journey. I can help people because it is a powerful story and it is a powerful journey.

My journey is far from over. I was sentenced by the court system to federal prison. I was charged in both state and federal court. The state system gave me probation but the federal system sentenced me with active time for my past crimes.

I was really frustrated when this happened. I didn't really understand at first that Light had removed me from this bondage but now I am being pulled back into these systems. I had already made real genuine changes in my life. Regardless of the sentence things will still be different this time. Light released me from the bondage and gave me an explosion of energy to get out her and help people that are suffering from mental illness, homelessness and addiction. I am going to use this opportunity of service to talk to others about everything I have seen and share with people who want to listen and listen to those who need to talk. Maybe I can help them.

I know this is a consequence of my actions. It is not always a happy story but it is part of my story. I worry about my family but I know Light will make sure they are taken care of.

Light released me from this bondage and made a promise to me that if I continue to reach out and share his message and my journey and my story that he will still be there for me. Light makes us promises and we know we will be taken care of. I feel like we run in to this same thing that Moses and Aaron did with the Pharoah whenever we are trying to make changes in the community by asking people in leadership roles to release the bondage from people that are suffering from addiction, mental health and other circumstances. Instead of locking them up in prisons, jails or institutions we could be trying to get them the help that they so desperately need. I know that will take a lot of policy change and reform but I have a lot of years left in my life therefore I feel like I have a lot of work to do.

The story of Moses is powerful. The story takes me back to August 28, 2019 when Light finally answered my prayers. I feel like it was not my time before and I was not ready. Light needed me to get where I was to be able to have this story and for it to be so powerful and genuine.

"Drugs really are great...but God is better."

Revelation

Revelation... John was visited by an angel sent by the Light. I think that this is a very important moment because immediately after this angel visits John, John drops to his knees to worship the angel but the angel corrects him because he is not Light. The angel tells John to let the fuckupers continue fuckingup and let the righteous continue to be righteous. "People can do whatever they want but the time is near and

Light is coming soon." So we are reminded that people who reject Light are going to find themselves separated from Light.

I am reminded that even though I was fuckingup for so long...the Light wiped me clean. It doesn't matter how much we do or don't do. Light is always there waiting for us. He is waiting to guide us. All we have to do is answer our calling from him and fulfill that calling. It is not enough just to accept Light as your guide. It is our responsibility as Lights to share the word of Light and be kind to one another especially to the outcasts.

I know in my heart one hundred percent that I am the Light...because the Light lives in me. Revelations tells us that we are all moving from Light to Light. I love it.

Light truly is the Way, the Truth and the Light.

Made in the USA
Coppell, TX
31 January 2022